Earthquake

Helen Adrienne Chapman · Illustrated by Mark Willenbrink

Contents

Rigby®

A Harcourt Achieve Imprint

www.Rigby.com
1-800-531-5015

Discovered in an Earthquake

Jack leaned against the elevator wall and whispered into his sister's ear. "I never thought I would complain about missing school, but I am not happy about Take Your Kids to Work Day."

"Even the word *seismologist* sounds boring," said Caryn, careful to keep her voice very quiet. "We'll just have to find some way to keep ourselves awake, because Dad's job is totally not cool."

The elevator stopped, and Jack and Caryn followed their dad into the Earthquake Information Center.

"What do you think?" Dad asked proudly, sweeping his hand toward a room full of blinking computers and very weird-looking graphs.

"Exciting, isn't it?" asked Dad, who didn't notice Jack and Caryn's gloomy faces.

Twenty minutes into their tour of the Center, Jack pulled at the back of Caryn's shirt, making her stop walking.

"Is it just me," he said quietly, "or does every room we've been in look exactly the same?"

Caryn whispered back, "I know, and if I see one more person staring at one more piece of equipment, I'm going to fall asleep."

Dad called out from down the hallway.

"You've seen everything now. Any questions?"

"I have a question, Dad," Caryn said. "In all of these rooms of fancy equipment, do you have a machine that can make me a snack?"

Dad laughed, saying, "Yes, as a matter of fact we do," and he pointed down the hall at a vending machine.

After buying Caryn and Jack muffins and juice, Dad led them to his office.

"So what's the point of watching all of this equipment all day?" asked Caryn as she brushed muffin crumbs off of her shirt.

"The equipment gives us information," explained Dad, "which we use to try to predict future quakes. We use a Richter scale to measure the earthquakes."

"How does the Richter scale . . . " began Caryn, but as she was talking her chair began to shake. "Cut it out, Jack!" she snapped, spinning around to glare at her brother, but he was on the other side of the room!

As a stapler began moving on Dad's desk, Caryn quickly realized that it wasn't just her chair—the whole building was shaking! Excitement swept through the Center, and Dad scooted his chair across the room to a computer in the corner.

"All of the equipment's going crazy," said Jack, as he looked out of the office at all of the beeping and blinking computers.

"It just looks that way," said Dad, "but every piece of equipment has a job to do."

He walked over to stand by Jack and began pointing around the room, saying, "See, this shows the size of the quake and how strong it is, and the other shows where the quake hit and . . . "

"Hey, guys," said Caryn, cutting in, "I don't mean to interrupt, but shouldn't we climb under a desk or something?"

"Don't worry, Caryn, we're in the safest place we could possibly be," said Dad. "Quakes push buildings from side to side, but the Center is built to be shockproof and hold up against any side pushes."

"This is so cool!" said Jack, who was moving around the room excitedly from machine to machine.

Fifteen seconds later it was all over, and nothing was shaking except for Caryn, who was trying not to show how much the earthquake had scared her.

Dad led Caryn and Jack into a meeting room with a large window.

"The quake hit miles away," said Dad, "but it was strong enough to cause damage here. Look, all of the traffic lights are stuck on red and the power lines are down."

Caryn and Jack pressed against the glass to see all of the damage that had been caused.

"Caryn, look at that old building that was knocked over," Jack said, pointing out the window at a large pile of bricks in the street.

"Dad, it looks like there's a fire down the street, but how would an earthquake have caused that?" Caryn asked.

"Gas pipes or electric cables must have cracked," explained Dad, "and that can quickly start a fire. The water pipes are probably broken, too, so the firefighters will just have to let the fires burn for now."

"This is kind of weird," said Jack. "I knew it was a big earthquake because I saw the measurements on the equipment, but to see real damage is scary."

"Yes," said Dad, "and all of that damage happened in just a few seconds."

Caryn suddenly gasped and turned and ran out of the room.

"What's wrong?" called Dad, as he chased her down the stairs and out into the street. She turned onto a street where a brick wall had fallen down and stopped near a skinny black dog who was barking and scratching at the pile of bricks.

"What are you doing?" Dad asked as he caught up to her.

"I'm sorry for running outside, but I think someone's trapped!" Caryn cried, her voice shaking.

"I saw emergency teams from the window—do you want me to go find one?" Jack asked Dad.

"Not yet. This could be a false alarm," Dad said as he began to slowly take some bricks off the pile.

"Hurry," pleaded Caryn.

"I'm afraid that if I rush, the bricks will move and harm what's underneath," Dad explained. "That's why rescue workers are always so careful." Brick by brick the pile grew smaller, and Dad stood up, saying, "Caryn, I don't think anything's here."

"Wait, I hear something," Caryn cried, and they looked down to see a dirty puppy peering at them from a hole in the pile. "Dad," Caryn said, "how could he survive when he was under so many bricks?"

"People often survive days of being trapped—all you need is an air pocket or a gap in the rubble," said Dad.

Caryn reached down and gently lifted the puppy out of the hole to safety.

"This pup and its mom look thin and hungry, so, unless someone claims them, I think they may need a home," Dad said.

Caryn cuddled the pup and said, "I'm going to call you Brick."

Jack petted the larger, skinny black dog and said, "And you can be Richter—Ric for short."

"I learned a lot today, Dad. Thanks for bringing us to work with you," Jack said as they walked toward the building.

"Me too," said Caryn, who had a dreamy look in her eyes as she continued, "and I think I want to be a seismologist when I grow up. I can picture it now: Caryn, the great seismologist, who studies earthquakes and rescues puppies. I don't think I have ever heard anything that sounds as cool as that!"

Movers and Shakers

If you don't live in an earthquake area, the thought of the earth shaking may seem strange. But in many places around the world, earthquakes strike all the time! However, most are so weak that we don't feel them.

The outer surface of the earth is divided into about 30 areas of rock called **tectonic plates**. These plates move very slowly, and most earthquakes happen where these plates meet.

The plates push rocks together or pull them apart along the **fault lines**. Rocks don't move easily, and great pressure must build up before they do. When rocks finally move, energy is released in the form of vibrations, and these vibrations create the **shock waves** of the earthquake.

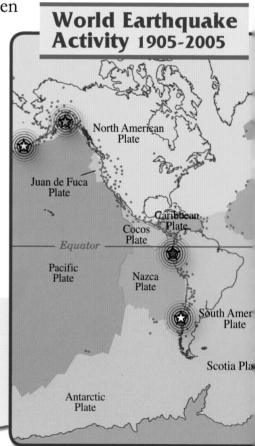

World Earthquake Activity 1905-2005

North American Plate

Juan de Fuca Plate

Caribbean Plate

Cocos Plate

Equator

Pacific Plate

Nazca Plate

South American Plate

Scotia Plate

Antarctic Plate

This map shows where some of the major earthquakes have occurred over the last hundred years. Which plate boundaries have been involved in the world's major earthquakes?

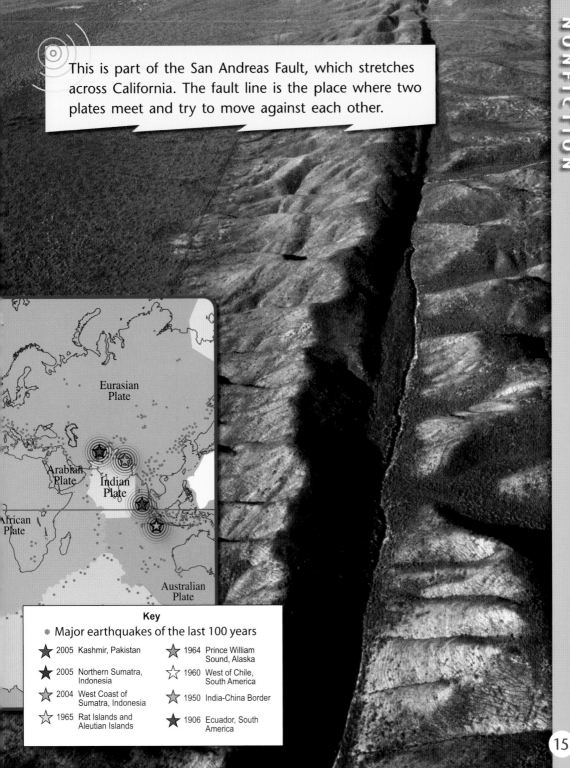

This is part of the San Andreas Fault, which stretches across California. The fault line is the place where two plates meet and try to move against each other.

Eurasian Plate

Arabian Plate

Indian Plate

African Plate

Australian Plate

Key

● Major earthquakes of the last 100 years

⭐ 2005 Kashmir, Pakistan

⭐ 2005 Northern Sumatra, Indonesia

⭐ 2004 West Coast of Sumatra, Indonesia

☆ 1965 Rat Islands and Aleutian Islands

⭐ 1964 Prince William Sound, Alaska

☆ 1960 West of Chile, South America

⭐ 1950 India-China Border

⭐ 1906 Ecuador, South America

Earthquake Damage

The effects of an earthquake are strongest in the area around the **epicenter**. The amount of damage to buildings and other structures depends on where the earthquake hits.

In rural areas, an earthquake can harm people, livestock, and crops. It can also destroy other plants and animals and their habitats.

When an earthquake hits a large city, it can cause deaths, injuries, and loss of property. A major earthquake can collapse city buildings, businesses, houses, factories, and bridges. It can also knock over power lines and trees.

How do you think an earthquake damaged this highway?

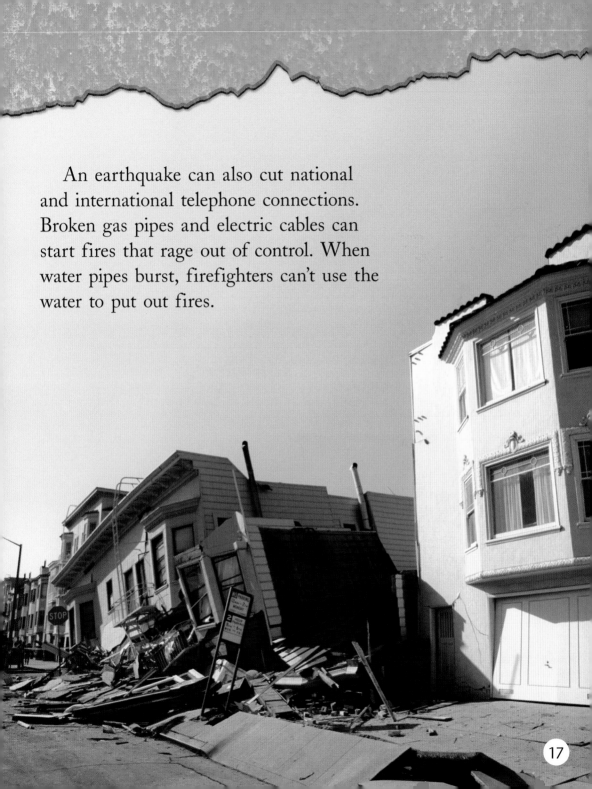

An earthquake can also cut national and international telephone connections. Broken gas pipes and electric cables can start fires that rage out of control. When water pipes burst, firefighters can't use the water to put out fires.

Millions of people can feel the shock waves of an earthquake. They might also feel its **aftershocks** or experience **tsunamis, landslides,** and floods that may follow the earthquake. Search and rescue teams save many people after an earthquake, but these people may still face homelessness, undrinkable water, and disease.

What kind of damage did this landslide cause?

Underwater Earthquakes

An earthquake can also happen under the sea, in the ocean floor. When this happens, it can sometimes cause a tsunami. The giant waves of a tsunami can travel very fast and can cause massive flooding.

How a Tsunami Forms

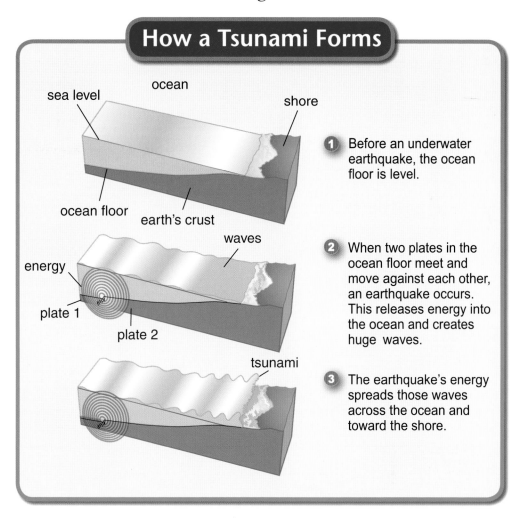

1 Before an underwater earthquake, the ocean floor is level.

2 When two plates in the ocean floor meet and move against each other, an earthquake occurs. This releases energy into the ocean and creates huge waves.

3 The earthquake's energy spreads those waves across the ocean and toward the shore.

How Scientists Measure Earthquakes

When rocks move along a fault, they make **seismic** waves that travel through the earth's crust and center. Seismic instruments can record even small waves on the other side of the world! These instruments are connected to a recording system called a seismometer. When an earthquake strikes, the part of the seismometer attached to the ground moves while the freely hanging part stays still. The difference in movement between the two parts is recorded and is usually displayed on a computer screen.

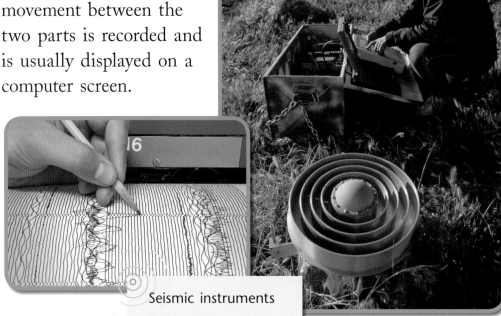

Seismic instruments

Off the Scales!

Scientists determine the size of an earthquake using a Richter scale. A Richter scale measures the energy released by earthquakes. The magnitude of an earthquake runs from −1 to 9 on this scale.

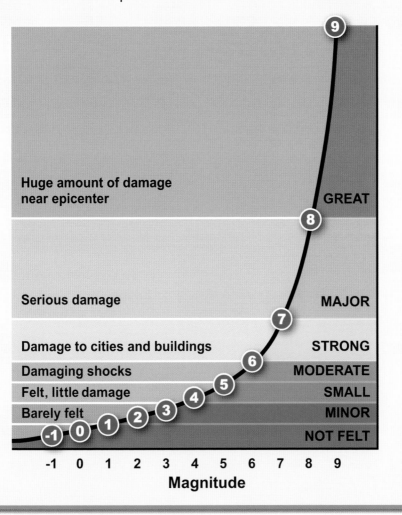

Huge amount of damage near epicenter — GREAT

Serious damage — MAJOR

Damage to cities and buildings — STRONG

Damaging shocks — MODERATE

Felt, little damage — SMALL

Barely felt — MINOR

NOT FELT

-1 0 1 2 3 4 5 6 7 8 9

Magnitude

Designed to Survive

No building is completely safe during an earthquake, but many countries have earthquake safety agencies that create rules to make buildings less likely to be damaged. Such buildings must:

- be built on a strong foundation
- survive an earthquake's sideways push
- be built of strong materials like metal and concrete

Scientists continue to study how the movement of the ground during earthquakes affects buildings. They can use what they learn to help design buildings and structures that can survive earthquake damage, not only in cities, but also in towns and rural communities around the world.

Which buildings in this photo do you think are most likely to withstand an earthquake?

What's Shaking?

In ancient times people thought huge animals, such as bears and snakes, lived deep under the ground. They believed these animals were so big that they shook the earth every time they moved! Over the years, there have been many inventions and discoveries that have helped in the study of earthquakes.

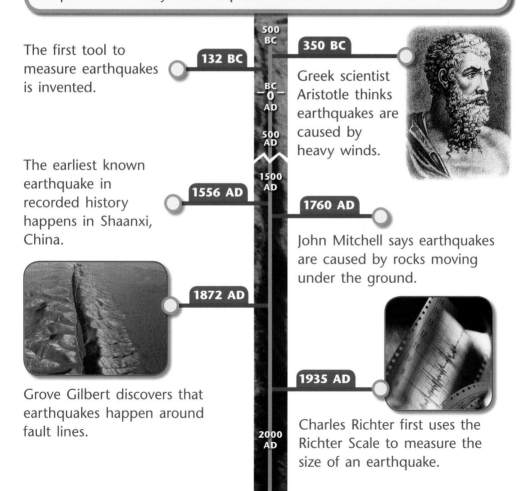

132 BC

The first tool to measure earthquakes is invented.

350 BC

Greek scientist Aristotle thinks earthquakes are caused by heavy winds.

1556 AD

The earliest known earthquake in recorded history happens in Shaanxi, China.

1760 AD

John Mitchell says earthquakes are caused by rocks moving under the ground.

1872 AD

Grove Gilbert discovers that earthquakes happen around fault lines.

1935 AD

Charles Richter first uses the Richter Scale to measure the size of an earthquake.

500 BC
BC 0 AD
500 AD
1500 AD
2000 AD

Glossary

aftershocks earthquakes that follow a major earthquake and are usually weaker in strength

epicenter the point on the earth's surface above where an earthquake started

fault lines cracks or breaks in a rock formed by the movement of the earth on either side of the cracks

landslides sudden rock or earth sliding down from mountain or cliff

seismic a word relating to vibrations and movements of the earth

shock waves sudden waves of pressure

tectonic plates solid pieces of the earth's crust which make up the surface of the earth

tsunamis high sea waves caused by an earthquake